THE WISE MEN
OF GOTHAM

The Wise Men of Gotham

ADAPTED AND ILLUSTRATED BY
Malcolm Carrick

THE VIKING PRESS · NEW YORK

FIRST AMERICAN EDITION

©Malcolm Carrick 1973. All rights reserved. Published in 1975 by The Viking Press, Inc., 625 Madison Avenue, New York, N.Y. 10022. Printed in U.S.A.

Library of Congress Cataloging in Publication Data. Carrick, Malcolm. The wise men of Gotham. Summary: Twelve folk tales featuring the people of Gotham, famous for their reputation of being born fools. A rewriting for children of the Mad men of Gotham. 1. Tales. [1. Folklore] I. Mad men of Gotham. II. Title. PZ8.1.C2273Wi [398.2] [E] 74–10832

ISBN 0–670–77520–7

1 2 3 4 5 79 78 77 76 75

Introduction

In rewriting these tales for children, I have used
as a guide the chap-book version of some stories which
first appeared in 1450 as *The Foles of Gotyam.*

Why then *The Wise Men of Gotham?*

The Oxford Dictionary of Nursery Rhymes tells how
the villagers of Gotham, thinking that where a King
had ridden thereafter became a Public road, stopped
King John from riding over their fields. The angry
King sent his servants to see the people of Gotham,
but when the servants arrived they found the villagers
doing all sorts of odd and foolish things, and they
returned to tell the King that Gotham was a Village
of Fools.

So the Men of Gotham kept their fields and a
reputation for being silly, although you might think
they were quite clever to have fooled King John.

MALCOLM CARRICK

The Cuckoo

THE PEOPLE of Gotham loved the spring. Every year they waited for the cold, hard winter to finish so that they could enjoy the long sunny days and dance and make merry.

"Oh, it's fine to be alive in Gotham in the spring," they would agree. But spring only comes once a year.

Now the wise men of Gotham would often meet to discuss such things as spring coming only once a year and why the sky was blue and how long is a piece of string. At one such meeting a wise fellow called Sillyfule had an idea.

"Spring comes when the cuckoo calls, and the cuckoo's disappearance means that summer is coming, then autumn, and

then the cold, hard winter." Everyone agreed that was very clever. "My idea is this: if we caught a cuckoo and kept it in Gotham all year, then spring would have to stay in Gotham, too."

The wise men all agreed that this was a brilliant plan. They decided to catch a cuckoo straightaway. Search parties were sent to the woods around Gotham to find a cuckoo and bring it back. When a cuckoo was caught, all Gotham was alive with the wonderful news.

"There will be no winter this year," they said, and some people even threw away their winter clothes.

The cuckoo was brought back in triumph and put in a cage. A small boy called Joe was to look after the bird. Well, the wise man's prediction came true: spring stayed in Gotham for a long time.

But then fruit started to blossom on the trees as it used to do in summer, and it got hotter.

"It's not exactly like spring," people thought, "but just as good," and they settled down to enjoy a whole year of spring.

The cuckoo, however, wasn't very happy; and Joe could see

that the bird wanted to fly away as he did every year, so one night he crept down to the cage and let the cuckoo free.

"Goodbye, cuckoo," he said.

The next morning everyone was aghast to find the cage empty. "The cuckoo's gone," they cried. "Spring will go now, then we shall have autumn and then winter."

It was too late to find another cuckoo.

"It's just as I feared," Sillyfule said at the next meeting of the wise men. "Without the cuckoo we'll have winter before the year's out, mark my words."

And he was right. Before Christmas, winter came to Gotham.

The Marriage Tale

THE PEOPLE of Gotham loved a wedding, and when Good Lot announced he was to marry, everyone gathered at the church in great excitement, because Good Lot was a very popular, well-mannered young man who always did as he was told; hence his name.

The service was very nice, and everyone was crying and smiling, when the priest said to Lot: "Now, Good Lot, say these things after me."

"These things after me," Good Lot replied solemnly.

"No, Lot," smiled the priest. "When I say repeat this, you have to repeat what I say."

Lot smiled and dutifully said, "You have to repeat what I say."

"Not me," said the priest impatiently, "you."

"You," replied Lot.

"No, not me. I'm not getting married, you are."

"No, not me. I'm not getting married, you are."

"Stop fooling around in church," the priest said angrily.

"Stop fooling around in church," Lot replied, thinking this was a very odd way to get married.

"You're a fool," cried the priest.

"You're a fool," cried Lot.

The people in the church gasped, and the priest stamped his foot and walked out, refusing to marry Good Lot. Everybody was amazed that Good Lot behaved so badly in church, and on his wedding day, too!

"He called the priest a fool," the people whispered to each other. Well, it was a long time before the priest had calmed down enough to try to marry Lot again, and when he did, he didn't say, "Good Lot, do you take this woman to be your wife?" He said, "You're a Bad Lot."

So ever after, when people thought someone was being naughty in church, they would say, "He's a bad lot."

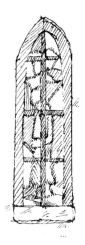

The Lazy Farmer's Tale

ONE DAY, a very lazy farmer called Farmer Sloth, who lived on a hill overlooking Gotham, was loading his cart with cheeses to take to the market.

"Every week it's the same," he moaned, "work, work, work. I wish I didn't have to pull these heavy cheeses all the way to the market." He moaned so much that he didn't look where he was putting them. One rolled off the cart, landed on its side, and kept rolling down the hill towards Gotham.

"Where are you going?" Farmer Sloth cried, and started to run after the cheese. Then he stopped and thought: "Why, that cheese is taking itself to market. Now I won't have to load it and haul it down the hill; I'll send them *all* that way." So he set the other cheeses rolling down the hill after the first. "I'll see you at the market," he cried gaily. "Now I can have a little sleep, then go and see who has bought my cheeses, and collect my money."

After his sleep, Farmer Sloth went down the hill. At the bottom there was a sharp curve in the road where another farmer lived: Farmer Woolize.

"Good morning Farmer Woolize," called Farmer Sloth gaily. "How is the world with you?"

"Very well," Farmer Woolize replied. "This morning I put my cows out, and they've turned all their milk to cheese." Sure enough, there were all the cheeses Farmer Sloth had sent down the hill. They had gone straight to Farmer Woolize's cows.

"They look rather like my cheeses," Farmer Sloth said, smiling. "But they can't be, because mine are at Gotham market."

Farmer Woolize was puzzled. "Then they must be from the cows; but what I don't understand is that their ankles are all bruised as if something had rolled into them."

"Probably the strain of making cheese." Farmer Sloth smiled. "Well, I must be off to market; no pulling that cart for me today."

When he arrived at the market, Farmer Sloth was surprised to find that nobody had seen his cheeses. He asked all the traders from one end of Gotham to the other.

"Have you bought my cheeses?"

"No," they all replied, "we haven't seen you or your cheeses today."

"What's happened to them, then?" fretted the farmer. "Perhaps the stupid cheeses kept rolling and went on to York. I'll have to go and see. It will be a hard walk, and I hate walking." But there was nothing for it. He had to walk all the way to York, and when he got there nobody had seen the cheeses, so he had to walk all the way back to Gotham; then from Gotham all the way home. So by the time he got to Farmer Woolize's farm, he was exhausted and miserable, and stopped to rest.

"I can't find those silly cheeses anywhere," he complained to his friend, "and I've done more work today than I ever do pulling the cart."

"It's a bad day all right," Farmer Woolize commiserated. "This morning, as you know, my cows laid dozens of cheeses, but now they only give milk."

"It's a sad day for both of us then," said Farmer Sloth as he struggled up the hill. And he resolved never to shirk his work again.

The Miller's Tale

EVERY WEEK the miller went to market to buy a sack of grain. He would saddle his horse at noon and ride over the bridge into the town, always arriving at one o'clock.

"It takes me just one hour to get to Gotham," he would say to the grain-seller, "but when I return home with my sack of grain, it takes me two hours, and I always miss my tea."

"Of course," the grain-seller replied, after thinking about the problem for a minute. "It takes longer because your horse has to carry you *and* the sack of grain."

The miller looked at the sack; it was very large and about as heavy as he was.

"Of course," he said, "if the grain weighs as much as I do, that is why it takes my horse twice as long to get home."

Well, when the time came for the miller to go home, as he stood by his horse saying goodbye to the grain-seller, he suddenly had a thought: "If my horse takes only one hour to get home with just me, and two hours to get home with me and the grain, the answer is simple: if someone else carries the grain, I'll be home in time for tea."

"Brilliant," said the grain-seller excitedly, "but who will carry it?"

"Why," the miller laughingly replied, "I don't mind a bit of extra work to get my tea; I'll carry it myself."

So the grain-seller put the grain on the miller's shoulders instead of across the horse's back, and the miller heaved himself into the saddle.

"Goodbye, you clever miller," waved the grain-seller, and the miller rode off home very unsteadily. But it still took him two hours to get home, and he missed his tea yet again.

The Alms Tale

WHEN LENT CAME to Gotham, as it came to everywhere else, the parish priest went round to his pious parishioners and asked them what they were going to give up for Lent. Now that year was very bad for the Gotham farmers. All the animals had already been sold, and all the crops had failed. Everyone was very, very poor; so when the priest came and asked the farmers what luxury they were going

to give up for Lent, the farmers couldn't think of anything.

"Well," the priest said, "why don't you give up eating two meals a day?"

"We would gladly," the farmers replied, "but we're lucky to have one meal a day."

"Well," the priest said, "you could give up drinking ale."

"We would gladly," they replied, "but we've got no money for ale, nor for food, so how can we give up something we haven't got?"

"How indeed," the priest mused. And whatever the pious farmers thought they would give up, when they thought about it they found they had nothing to give up.

Lent came, and everybody was worried. The villagers all went to the priest with deep frowns on their faces.

"I've an idea," the priest told them. "Instead of giving something up for Lent, you can give alms to the poor. Give me all your money, and I will give it to the poor people."

"What a clever idea," they all said, and, digging into their pockets, they brought out all the money they had. It was hardly enough to buy them a meal that day, but they parted with it gladly, for they were good people.

"Now," the priest said, "I'll go and give this money to the poorest people in Gotham, and then we shall all go to church together."

Well, the farmers waited for the priest to find the poorest people in Gotham and give them the money. He was gone for a long time, and when he came back he still had the money in his hand.

"What's the matter?" asked the farmers, anxiously.

The priest scratched his head and said, "It would appear that you farmers are the poorest people in Gotham, so take this money, and distribute it amongst yourselves."

The farmers did so, and they went to church well content: not only had they given alms to the poor for Lent, but it hadn't cost them a penny.

The Blacksmith's Tale

IN GOTHAM VILLAGE there was a large stable with a forge where people came to have new shoes put on their horses. The blacksmith was a jolly fellow called Blacksmith Blacksmith. Because he got very dirty from the fire, people called him Black, and as his father's name was Smith, people called him Smith, and as he was a blacksmith, people called him Blacksmith Blacksmith. But some people just called him Dick for short.

One summer, some wasps made a nest in the stable straw, much to the annoyance of Blacksmith Blacksmith's customers. The wasps stung the horses, making them bolt and run away;

and they stung the customers, making them angry and sore, but they never bothered Blacksmith Blacksmith because he was always working near the hot fire. Well, the customers were soon tired of being stung, and stopped coming to the forge.

"We'd rather go to Nottingham than be stung," they said.

Soon Blacksmith Blacksmith had no money to pay his rent. When the squire came round, Blacksmith Blacksmith said sadly, "I'm afraid I can't pay my rent. It's not my fault; I've lost all my customers because the wasps in the straw sting them. Please don't take away my stable and forge; they're all I have in the world."

"You Blacksmith clot!" retorted the squire. "Get rid of the wasps, and your customers will come back. Then they'll pay you,

you can pay your rent, and I will let you stay here."

Blacksmith Blacksmith thanked the squire for his good advice, and went inside to get rid of the wasps. "But how?" he pondered. Blacksmith Blacksmith looked hard at the forge. What could he use to get rid of the wasps?

"I could shoe them all, then they'd be too heavy to fly," he thought. "No, that would never do, I haven't got small enough shoes. Perhaps I could put blinkers on them – such large ones that they couldn't see where they were flying? No."

While he was thinking, he went to the fire to get out his irons, which were growing too hot. "Of course!" He jumped and kicked himself for being so silly. "If the wasps avoid the fire for fear of being burnt, I'll set the straw alight to prevent them staying there."

So he plunged his red-hot iron into the straw, which leapt into flames and, sure enough, out flew the wasps; but they just buzzed around the rafters, so Blacksmith Blacksmith made another fire *there*. Then the wasps moved near the door, so Blacksmith Blacksmith, not to be swayed from his plan by cunning insects, lit a fire there, too. Only when the whole place was on fire did the wasps fly out of the door, never to be seen again. As the raging fire brought the forge to the ground, Blacksmith Blacksmith explained to everyone how he had at last got rid of the wasps.

"How clever," the people cried. "He's burnt them out. Now we'll be able to have our horses shod in peace."

"And I'll be able to pay my rent," the blacksmith added. But the villagers still had to go to Nottingham to have their horses shod, because Blacksmith Blacksmith had completely burnt down the forge.

"Still," he laughed to his friends, "if there's no forge, I cannot pay rent, can I? Then with the money I save I shall buy a new forge." Everyone was astounded at his cleverness, and because Blacksmith Blacksmith didn't have to work any more, and still saved money, everyone called him Blacksmith Cleverdick. Everyone except the squire, that is.

The Four Silly Brothers

ONCE THERE WERE four brothers: Matthew, Mark, Luke and John. One day, as they returned home from work, they talked and sang and remembered what a fine day it had been. Suddenly the eldest brother, Matthew, stopped and said, "Are we all here?"

"Why," the others replied, "of course."

"Are you sure?" The eldest brother looked at the others. "I'd better count just to make sure." So he did. "One, two, three," he

counted. "There, I told you someone was missing. We are four brothers, yet I can only count three. Someone is still in the fields." The next brother, Mark, said, "Wait a minute, let *me* count." And he counted the other brothers. "One, two, three. Oh dear! One of us is lost. We must find him."

As they rushed off in a great panic, the third brother, Luke, who was good at counting sheep and generally very clever, stopped them. "I'll count," he said, and he did so very carefully. "One, two, three . . . Oh quick! Let's go and find our lost brother before night falls." Off they went, searching and calling for their lost brother until the sun started to go down. John, the

youngest brother, was beside himself with grief. "Let me count again before we have to go and tell the sad news to our parents. One, two, three . . . only three."

The four brothers were standing in the road, wailing and bemoaning the loss of their brother, when a gentleman rode up. "What's all this?" he asked.

"We've lost our brother," Matthew, Mark, Luke and John all cried together. "There were four of us this morning, and now we're only three."

"Three?" said the gentleman. "How do you work that out?"

"Look," said Matthew impatiently, and he counted his other brothers. "One, two, three."

The gentleman smiled as he saw the foolish brothers were not including themselves as they counted. "How much will you give me if I find your other brother?" the gentleman asked.

"All our money," cried the brothers, and eagerly opened their purses.

"Well then," said the gentleman, taking the money and getting out his cudgel, "Stand here in a line." The brothers did so, and the gentleman bashed them all over the head.

"ONE, TWO, THREE, FOUR! You silly brothers, you forgot to count yourselves!" So, laughing and counting his new-found wealth, the gentleman rode off.

The brothers were very happy to find that they were not lost
after all. They waved their thanks to the gentleman,
and set off home holding their heads and counting
their bumps, ONE, TWO, THREE, FOUR.

The Hare

EVERY YEAR in Gotham, the men who rented the farms and shops and houses had to pay their rents to the squire of Gotham. The rent had to be paid on the first day of April, or the men of Gotham would be thrown off their land by the pitiless squire who never laughed or joked, but was always scowling and miserable. So every year on the last day of March the fastest runner in Gotham, who was known as Jack the Runner, collected all the rents and ran as fast as he could to the squire's house to pay them. The squire's house was a long way from Gotham, so Jack had to run very fast to get there before April the first.

"Our Jack can run nearly as fast as a hare," the villagers would say. They all agreed it was a great fortune to have such a fine runner living in Gotham.

Well, this particular year, spring was beautiful in Gotham village. The birds were singing and the trees were in blossom and everyone was so happy that they forgot about paying the rent. Suddenly Jack the Runner realised that March had gone and it was April the first and the rents had not been paid.

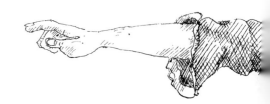

"Oh dear," cried the shopkeepers and the farmers and the householders, as Jack ran round collecting the rents together. But by the time he had collected them, the sun was high in the sky.

"It's no good," Jack said. "I'll never reach the squire's house by the end of the day." The villagers gathered together to decide what to do. No one could think of anything until a very wise man spoke up.

"I know someone who can run faster than Jack," he said.

"Who?" cried the villagers.

"Why, my pet hare. He could reach the squire's house in half a day."

Everything was soon settled. The wise man got his hare, and all the villagers listened while Jack told the hare the fastest way to the squire's house. Then he put a bag of gold, which was to pay the rents, around the hare's neck and let him go. But the hare didn't follow Jack's route. He scampered back to the woods where the wise man first caught him. The silly villagers said:

"Ah, that's a clever hare; he must be going a quick way that Jack doesn't know about."

So they went back to enjoying the spring, thinking that their rent had been paid by the hare.

The squire, meanwhile, was still waiting for the rent, and when he heard that the villagers had put it round the neck of a hare to deliver, he fell about with laughter. He was so happy to be able to share a joke after being so miserable, he never told the Gotham people that their rents hadn't been paid that year.

The Wives' Tale

ALMOST EVERY day in Gotham the wives of the town would
meet in the ale-house for a chat and a drink. They always
talked about how well they looked after their husbands,
and how clever they were at saving money.

"Why," the first wife would say, "instead of wasting my time
baking and brewing for my husband, if I have a spare moment I
pray that he will have enough bread and ale."

"Very commendable," the second would agree. "I, too, save
my husband money, because I never light candles when it gets
dark, but send everyone to bed."

"That's an idea," the third would nod. "I save housekeeping
money by sitting here all day and never doing the shopping, and
it only costs me half as much."

"How very clever," the fourth wife said. "I save my husband's

coal. Instead of lighting a nice fire in my house, I go to other people's houses and chat all day."

The fifth wife told how she, too, was industrious and saved money.

"Instead of weaving flax and wool into warm clothes for the children, I save it all in a drawer."

The sixth wife told how she always stayed late at other people's houses, so that instead of her husband talking to her, he saved his breath.

"I save money on meat," the seventh wife said. "Instead of buying pork and beef I buy pigs and cows, which are cheaper, although it does cost a bit to feed them."

But all the wives agreed that the innkeeper's wife was the most industrious of them all. She saved her husband a fortune every week. "Yes," the wife of the innkeeper would say, giving all her friends some more ale. "If it wasn't for me and my friends drinking all my husband's beer, it would surely go sour."

The Sack of Grain

EVERY MONTH in Gotham there was a market. Everyone came from miles around to buy and sell food and animals; everything you could imagine. On the way into Gotham they had to pass over a small wooden bridge, and sometimes it got very crowded and the travellers had to wait a long time to cross. Well, one market day a shepherd came from Gotham to the bridge. He had been to see if the price of sheep was high,

and now he was returning home to fetch his sheep. On the other side of the bridge was another shepherd who was going on his way to Gotham to buy some sheep. As they crossed the bridge the first shepherd said to the second shepherd, "Hello there! Where are you going?"

"I'm going to buy some sheep and bring them home," the second shepherd replied.

"Well," said the first shepherd, "you'd better find another way to come home because I'm going to get my sheep to sell in the

market, and I shall bring them over this bridge, so there won't be room for your sheep, too."

"Nonsense," said the second shepherd indignantly. "Why should I find another route? It's *you* who should go another way."

"No, you," cried the first.

"You," shouted the second. They argued so fiercely that they came to blows and were fighting fiercely when a miller came to the bridge, carrying a sack of grain he had just bought in the market.

"Stop! Stop fighting!" he implored the shepherds. Eventually he separated them and listened while they told him why they were fighting. When the miller heard what they had been fighting about, he laughed and laughed.

"Why are you laughing?" demanded the shepherds.

"Because you're fighting over something that isn't there," he laughed.

"That's true," said the first shepherd.

"Nonsense!" cried the second.

"How foolish you are," said the miller. "I'll show you. I have

a good sack of grain here that I would fight for: now look." The miller poured the grain over the bridge into the river. "Do you see, you stupid fellows: now I have no grain I have nothing to fight over, have I?"

"Certainly not," agreed the shepherds.

"Yet that is what you were doing," the miller explained patiently. "Fighting over nothing."

The two shepherds saw how silly they had been and, thanking the miller for his good sense, they parted friends.

Now, who was the silliest man on the bridge?

Why, the miller of course. He had lost his sack of grain, while the shepherds had lost nothing.

The Cheese

ONE DAY a man from Gotham was riding home through the woods for his dinner. He was very hungry. "I wouldn't mind a bite to eat right now," he thought, and, much to his surprise, as he glanced down at the road, there was a large, yellow cheese which had fallen from a cart on its way to Gotham market. He edged his horse carefully towards it and gleefully took out his sword so that he could pick it up. But the sword was too short, and no matter how he twisted and turned he could not reach the cheese.

"Well, there is nothing else for it," the man decided. "I'll just have to pop into Gotham and get another sword, a longer one." So off he went, and after much bargaining and measuring with the swordsmith he bought a longer sword and rode back to the place in the woods where the cheese still lay.

"Oh, cheeses!" cried the man angrily. "I didn't buy a long enough sword." So he returned to the swordsmith, the thought of the scrumptious cheese making him hungrier and hungrier. This time he swapped the sword he had for the longest sword in the shop. It was so long that it dragged along the ground and he could hardly remount his horse. "My dinner will be ruined by now," he moaned. "Still, I shall have that lovely cheese."

Soon he was back in the woods, and the cheese was still lying there in the middle of the road. Once again he leant and twisted and turned, and this time his sword just touched the cheese, but

still it wouldn't go far enough for him to be able to pick it up.

Just then another man rode up. He, too, was going home for his dinner, and he, too, was hungry. "Whatever are you doing, Gotham man?" he inquired.

"What do you think I'm doing? I'm trying to reach this cheese, but my sword isn't long enough, and I can't think of any other way to reach it," the man with the sword explained patiently.

"You are a silly fellow," commented the second man. "If you want that cheese as much as I do, all you have to do is get off your horse and pick it up." Which is exactly what the other fellow did. He picked up the cheese, got back on his horse and rode off.

"Of course," the silly fellow thought. "All I have to do is to get off my horse and pick up the cheese; I didn't need a sword at all." But as soon as he got off his horse he realised that the other fellow had already taken the cheese.

"So I'm left with nothing but a very long sword and a very burnt dinner."

The Fish Tale

GOTHAM PEOPLE liked fish, and the fishmongers of Gotham were always busy buying and selling fish, but sometimes there were some left over. They couldn't be kept because they soon went bad, but it seemed a shame to throw away perfectly good fish. One fishmonger had an idea about left-over fish, and called a meeting of the fishmongers.

"Why don't we put the fish into Gotham pond? There they can breathe as they do in the sea, and in a year's time we shall have a fine lot of fish without having to pay for them."

All the fishmongers thought this was a wonderful idea. One fellow thought it would be better to put the fish back in the sea but, as the fishmonger with the idea pointed out, it might be difficult to catch them again, as the sea is somewhat larger than Gotham pond. Well, every time the fishmongers had any sprats, red herrings, smoked salmon or kippers left over from the

day's trade, they would gaily fling them into the pond, and lick their lips at the thought of all the fish keeping so nicely there.

On All Fools' Day, a great feast was to be held in Gotham, and the fishmongers were asked to contribute some fish. "Why not some fish from the pond?" they thought, and they got their rods and nets and went down to Gotham pond. At first they were most surprised to be catching nothing. "It must be full of fish," they argued, and continued fishing. Suddenly the largest net buckled and bent.

"A catch!" they cried and, dropping all their other lines, they rushed to pull in the big net. When they had landed their

catch, everyone gasped. It was not full of fine eating-fish, but one huge eel. "That's why there are no good eating-fish in the pond," the fishmongers told each other. "The eel must have eaten them all to have grown so huge. Let's eat *him*," they cried angrily, reaching for their knives.

"Wait," said the fishmonger with the idea. "There may be other eels in the pond. In order to show them what we think of them, let's take this eel to the river and drown it."

So, with grim faces and grave mutterings, the fishmongers took the eel to the river and drowned it. And the eel didn't mind a bit.

The End Tale

This tale is too silly for words:
so I haven't written any!